Reproducible Activities

Using the Standards

Building Grammar & Writing Skills

Grade 1

By

Q. L. Pearce

Published by Instructional Fair • TS Denison
an imprint of

 **Children's Publishing**

Author: Q. L. Pearce
Editors: Jeanine Manfro, Stephanie Oberc, Christine Hood

 **Children's Publishing**

Published by Instructional Fair • TS Denison
An imprint of McGraw-Hill Children's Publishing
Copyright © 2003 McGraw-Hill Children's Publishing

Send all inquiries to:
McGraw-Hill Children's Publishing
3195 Wilson Drive NW
Grand Rapids, Michigan 49544

Using the Standards: Building Grammar & Writing Skills—Grade 1
ISBN: 0-7424-1801-4

1 2 3 4 5 6 7 8 9 PHXBK 07 06 05 04 03

Introduction

Communication skills, both written and verbal, are critical in today's society. Before entering the school system, children have a general concept of structure and grammar; however, continued success in school is dependent on children's general knowledge of basic grammar and writing skills. In this book, we will build on that foundation through the use of activities designed specifically to reflect English Language Standards defined by the NCTE and IRA.

Because standards teaching and testing are at an all-time high, it is important that children not only understand the basics of grammar and writing, but also how to demonstrate their knowledge through testing and assessment. This book includes over 100 activities that provide further progress with basic skills in grammar and writing essential for future academic success. From alphabet review to creative writing and poetry, individual activities enhance curriculum, while offering flexibility and practice in each area.

For your convenience, you will find an overview of the 12 English Language Arts Standards (page 4), as well as an expanded Table of Contents (pages 5–8), which is organized into three easy-to-read columns. The first column lists the title of each activity. The second column lists the numbers of the NCTE standards addressed by the activity. Any one activity may address one or several standards. Page numbers where you can find the activities are listed in the third column.

This book is divided into seven sections, according to skills: Basic Grammar Skills, Capitalization, Punctuation, Parts of Speech, Usage, Writing Strategies, and Writing Applications. Some activities are simple, while others are more challenging. All activities, however, are designed to guide the grade one student to a basic understanding of the English language and the writing process. A comprehensive Answer Key is located at the back of the book, beginning on page 124.

© McGraw-Hill Children's Publishing

English Language Arts Standards

1. Read a wide range of texts.

2. Read a wide range of literature.

3. Apply a variety of strategies to comprehend and interpret texts.

4. Use spoken, written, and visual language to communicate effectively.

5. Use a variety of strategies while writing and use elements of the writing process to communicate.

6. Apply knowledge of language structure and conventions, media techniques, figurative language, and genre to create, critique, and discuss texts.

7. Research issues and interests, pose questions, and gather data to communicate discoveries.

8. Work with a variety of technological and other resources to collect information and to communicate knowledge.

9. Understand and respect the differences in language use across cultures, regions, and social roles.

10. Students whose first language is not English use their first language to develop competencies in English and other content areas.

11. Participate in a variety of literary communities.

12. Use spoken, written, and visual language to accomplish purposes.

0-7424-1801-4 Building Grammar & Writing Skills

© McGraw-Hill Children's Publishing

0-7424-1801-4 Building Grammar & Writing Skills

Table of Contents	Standards Reflected	Page

Usage

© McGraw-Hill Children's Publishing 0-7424-1801-4 Building Grammar & Writing Skills

Table of Contents	Standards Reflected	Page
Part II: Writing Strategies		
Simple Subjects	3, 4, 6	80
It's All in the Action	3, 4, 6	81
Complete Sentences	3, 4, 6	82
It's Not Finished	3, 4, 6	83
Crack the Code	3, 4, 5, 6	84
Tell All About It	3, 4, 6	85
I'm Asking	3, 4, 6	86
Telling or Asking	3, 4, 6	87
Make a Change	3, 4, 5, 6, 12	88
Mix and Match	3, 4, 5, 6, 12	89
Word Scramble	3, 4, 5, 6, 12	90
What's the Idea?	3, 4, 6	91
The Main Idea	3, 4, 6	92
Patrick's Present	3, 4, 5, 6	93
Lining Up	3, 4, 6	94
Costume Party	4, 6	95
Finding Groups	4, 6	96
What Doesn't Belong?	4, 6	97
Ringed Seals	3, 4, 6	98
Movie Mania	3, 4, 5, 6	99
In the End	3, 4, 5, 6	100
Scrambled Sentences	3, 4, 5, 6	101
Fact Find	1, 3, 4, 5, 6, 7	102
Organize an Outline	4, 5, 6, 7, 12	103
Part III: Writing Applications		
All About Insects	3, 4, 5, 6, 7	104
Dear Friend	4, 5, 6, 12	105
Thank You!	4, 5, 6, 12	106
My Story	3, 4, 5, 6, 7, 11, 12	107
What Do You Think?	3, 4, 6, 7, 8	108
Dear Diary	4, 5, 6, 12	109
Write It Right	1, 3, 4, 6	110
And Then . . .	3, 4, 5, 6, 7, 12	111
Imagine Who	4, 5, 6, 7, 12	112
Imagine Where	4, 5, 6, 12	113
Point of View	3, 4, 6, 8	114
What Comes Next?	3, 4, 6, 7, 8	115
Telling a Story	4, 5, 6, 7, 8, 12	116
A Beautiful Walk	1, 3, 4, 5, 6, 12	117
The Lost Shoe	4, 5, 6, 7, 8, 12	118

© McGraw-Hill Children's Publishing

0-7424-1801-4 Building Grammar & Writing Skills

Table of Contents	Standards Reflected	Page
Animal Tale	4, 5, 6, 7, 12	119
A Good Day	3, 4, 5, 6, 7, 12	120
Magic and Mystery	1, 3, 4, 5, 6, 7, 12	121
Write a Cinquain	2, 4, 5, 6, 11, 12	122
Rollicking Rhymes	2, 4, 5, 6, 11, 12	123
Answer Key		**124**

0-7424-1801-4 Building Grammar & Writing Skills

Name _____ Date _____

Cuddly Kitty

Connect the dots to finish the picture.
Begin with the letter **A**.
Follow the alphabet to **Z**.
Then color the picture.

0-7424-1801-4 Building Grammar & Writing Skills

Name _____ Date _____

Alphabet Soup

Write the letters of the alphabet in order.
Some of the letters are in this alphabet soup.

A

0-7424-1801-4 Building Grammar & Writing Skills

Name _____ Date _____

ABC Order

Write the words from the word box in ABC order.
Match the first letter of each word with the alphabet letter.

Word Box

apple	wish	jump	nut	top	king
zebra	under	hat	cup	girl	oak
van	x-ray	duck	boy	moon	seed
rat	egg	quick	lip	fish	pen
ice	you				

apple b c d

e f g h

i j k l

m n o p

q r s t

u v w x

y z

0-7424-1801-4 Building Grammar & Writing Skills

Name _____ Date _____

Order, Please!

Write each set of words in ABC order.
Use the first letter of each word.

Example: ant, bear, cup

dog   cat   bear

1. _____

2. _____

3. _____

egg   bird   leaves

1. _____

2. _____

3. _____

lizard   alligator   gecko

1. _____

2. _____

3. _____

wind   snow   rain

1. _____

2. _____

3. _____

0-7424-1801-4 Building Grammar & Writing Skills

Name _____ Date _____

Next in Line

Write each set of words in ABC order.
Use the <u>second</u> letter of each word.

Example: bag, big, bug

cap   cone   clown

1. _____

2. _____

3. _____

fairy   fish   feast

1. _____

2. _____

3. _____

moon   milk   mud

1. _____

2. _____

3. _____

stare   spoon   swan

1. _____

2. _____

3. _____

0-7424-1801-4 Building Grammar & Writing Skills

Name _____ Date _____

In the Beginning

Most of the letters of the alphabet are consonants.
They can come at the beginning of words.
Look at the picture.
Choose consonants from the beach balls to complete the words.

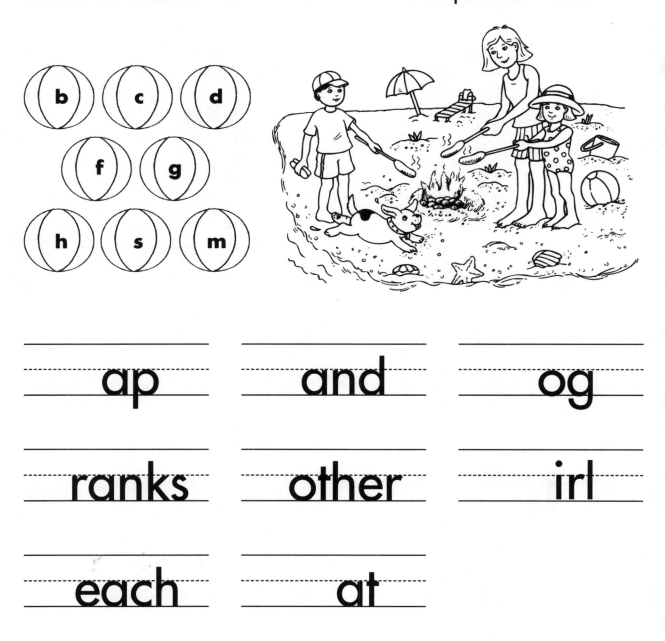

__ ap   __ and   __ og

__ ranks   __ other   __ irl

__ each   __ at

0-7424-1801-4 Building Grammar & Writing Skills

Name _____ Date _____

Lots of Letters

The items in the shopping cart are missing their beginning letters. Choose consonants from the apples to complete the words.

____ orn   ____ ettuce   ____ una

____ oodles   ____ opcorn   ____ aisins

____ read   ____ ilk

0-7424-1801-4 Building Grammar & Writing Sk

Name _____ Date _____

Spelling Test

Look at Tina's spelling word list.
The first letter from each word is missing.
Choose consonants from the pencils to complete the words.

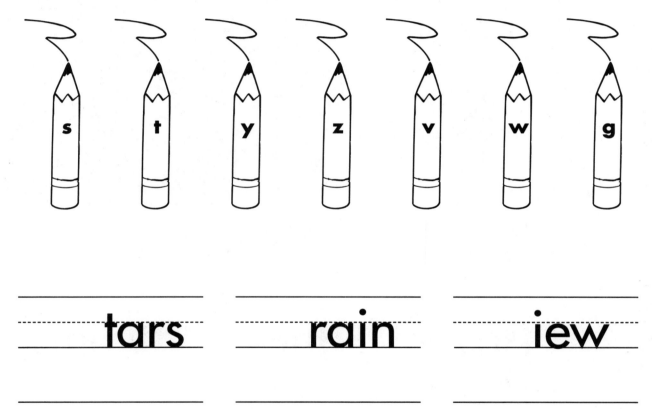

____tars	____rain	____iew
____agon	____-ray	____ellow
____oo	____ive	

0-7424-1801-4 Building Grammar & Writing Skills

Name _____ Date _____

Ending Consonants

Each shirt is missing the last letter of a boy's name.
Choose consonants from the basketballs to complete the names.

Rober _____ Davi _____ Jef _____

Chri _____ Jorda _____ Tro _____

Dar _____ Ma _____

   0-7424-1801-4 Building Grammar & Writing Skills

Name _____ Date _____

At Last

The ending consonant is missing from each word below.
Draw a line from the picture to the correct ending consonant.

pa   k

cla   x

skun   t

ba   r

fo   n

gir   p

flowe   l

0-7424-1801-4 Building Grammar & Writing Skills

Name _____ Date _____

Teamwork Tree

Some letters work together as a "team."
Together they make one sound.
Look at the letter pairs on the tree.
Then read the words and underline the letter pairs.

1. skunk

2. crayon

3. tree

4. snake

5. broom

6. crab

7. brush

8. skate

9. truck

10. pretty

© McGraw-Hill Children's Publishing

0-7424-1801-4 Building Grammar & Writing Skills

Name _____ Date _____

Perfect Pairs

Look at each picture.
Fill in the missing letter pair to complete each word.

fl   bl   pl   cl   sl

1. _____ our

2. _____ ay

3. _____ ag

4. _____ ock

5. _____ ide

6. _____ ed

7. _____ ock

8. _____ ant

9. _____ imb

20

0-7424-1801-4 Building Grammar & Writing Skills

Name _____ Date _____

Pairing Up

Some letter pairs can be at the beginning or at the end of words.
Read the words on the clock.
Circle the letter pairs.
Be sure to look at the beginning and the end of each word.

sh   ch   th

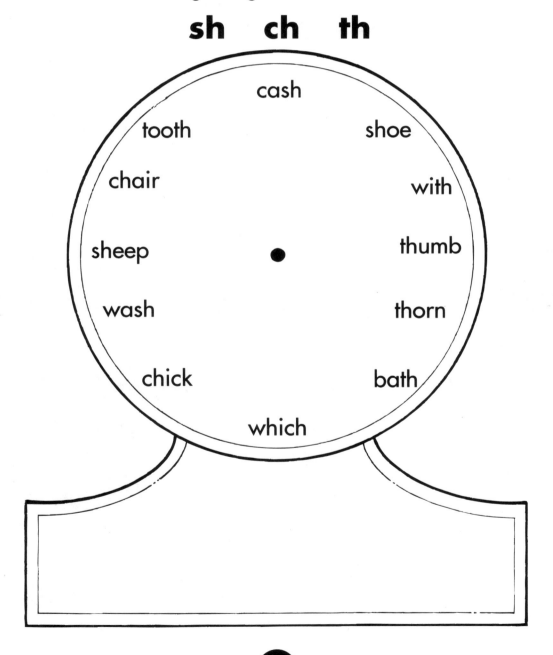

0-7424-1801-4 Building Grammar & Writing Skills

Name _____ Date _____

Building with Long Vowels

The letters **a**, **e**, **i**, **o**, and **u** are vowels.
They can make different sounds.
Long vowels say their own names.

Choose long vowel words from the word box.
Write them on the blocks in the wall.

Word Box

leg	knee	cake	bone	hat
time	ton	cup	pick	use

0-7424-1801-4 Building Grammar & Writing Skills

Name _____ Date _____

At the Zoo

The names of some of the zoo animals have long vowels.
Color these animals.

zebra   ape   giraffe

lion   snake   deer

fox   panda   tiger

0-7424-1801-4 Building Grammar & Writing Skills

Name _____ Date _____

Short Vowel Search

Some vowels have short sounds.
Circle the picture in each row that has a short vowel sound.
Hint: There may be more than one!

Example:

1.

2.

3.

4.

5.

24

0-7424-1801-4 Building Grammar & Writing Skills

Name _____ Date _____

Name Game

Some of these children's names have long vowels.
Color their shirts blue.
Some of these children's names have short vowels.
Color their shirts green.

0-7424-1801-4 Building Grammar & Writing Skills

Name _____   Date _____

Sneaky, Silent E

The letter **e** at the end of a word can change a short vowel to a long vowel. The **e** is silent.

Example: not + e = note

Add an **e** to each word on the left to make a new word.
Write the new words on the lines.

1. cut _____

2. mop _____

3. can _____

4. pan _____

5. bit _____

6. tub _____

7. kit _____

8. cub _____

Name _____ Date _____

Fishing for Capitals

Kevin is fishing for capital letters.
Color the fish that have capital letters.

0-7424-1801-4 Building Grammar & Writing Skills

Name _____ Date _____

Starting a Sentence

The first word in a sentence begins with a capital letter.
Read the sentences.
Write the first word in each sentence with a capital letter.

1. (the) _____ flower smells very nice.

2. (anne) _____ has a black kitten.

3. (do) _____ you like to play baseball?

4. (where) _____ is your pen?

5. (fruit) _____ is a good snack.

6. (turn) _____ on the light.

7. (blue) _____ is my favorite color.

8. (my) _____ room is very small.

9. (rain) _____ helps flowers grow.

10. (alan) _____ has a pony.

28

Name _____ Date _____

Capital Reports

Names of specific people, places, and titles of respect start with a capital letter. **Example: Mr.** and **Mrs.** are titles of respect.

Look at these reports.
The names of people and places aren't capitalized.
For each report, circle the letters that should be capitalized.
Then rewrite each report cover correctly.

rocky mountains
by
ms. clair thomas

main street
by
mr. raymond ross

  0-7424-1801-4 Building Grammar & Writing Skills

Name _____ Date _____

Capital Craze

Use capital letters for titles of books, poems, magazines, and movies.

> **Hint:** Unless they are the first word in a title, you don't have to capitalize these little words: at, by, for, in, of, to, with, and, but, or, a, an, the.

Examples: Little Red Riding Hood
The Wind in the Willows
Baseball Magazine

Rewrite each title using correct capitalization.

1. Poem
jack and jill
_____
_____

2. Magazine
sports digest
_____
_____

3. Book
favorite tales
_____
_____

4. Book
old yeller
_____
_____

5. Movie
monsters, inc.
_____
_____

6. Movie
cats and dogs
_____
_____

30

Name _____ Date _____

Calendar Capitals

Months, days of the week, and holidays begin with a capital letter. Look at Kyle's plans for the month of November. Circle the letters that should be capitals.

1. the science report is due monday.

2. tom's birthday is november 4.

3. see dr. platt on wednesday.

4. soccer practice is changed to thursday.

5. our pizza party is on saturday.

6. make crafts for thanksgiving.

0-7424-1801-4 Building Grammar & Writing Skills

Name _____ Date _____

Capital Review

Read the paragraph.
Circle the letters that should be capitals.
Hint: You should find 25 mistakes.

jenna's special day

jenna loves to swim. last thursday she went with her dad to clarefield water park. they took her best friend elena. it was very crowded. it was fourth of july weekend. elena takes swimming lessons from mr. hernandez. she showed Jenna a new stroke. they ate lunch at pirate pete's cove. Jenna had lots of fun. she wants to go back in august.

0-7424-1801-4 Building Grammar & Writing Skills

Name _____ Date _____

That's the Point

A **period (.)** is used at the end of a sentence that tells something or gives a command.

Read the sentences.
Put a period at the end of each sentence that tells something or gives a command.

Examples: **Telling Sentence:** I am happy.
Command: Please do your homework.

1. Please sit down

2. John is tired

3. Did you see your sister

4. Eat your dinner

5. Why is Taylor running

6. That mouse ate all the cheese

7. My friends sang a birthday song

8. I like dinosaurs

9. Please answer the telephone

10. Are you hungry

0-7424-1801-4 Building Grammar & Writing Skills

Name _____ Date _____

Short and Sweet

Some long words can be written as abbreviations.
An **abbreviation** is a shorter way to write a word.
It has a period at the end.

Examples: Doctor—Dr.
January—Jan.

Read the sentences.
Underline each abbreviation.
Then circle the word at the end of each sentence that is abbreviated.

1. Nick took his new puppy to see Dr. Jinah.   (Doctor   Driver)
2. Mr. Tate is our bus driver.   (Master   Mister)
3. My birthday is Jan. fifth.   (July   January)
4. Thurs. Tina has band practice.   (Thursday   Tuesday)
5. Main St. is the center of town.   (Strand   Street)

Put a period after these abbreviations for days of the week.
Then draw a line to match the abbreviations to the words they
stand for.

Sun	Thursday
Mon	Sunday
Tues	Saturday
Wed	Monday
Thurs	Friday
Fri	Tuesday

34

    0-7424-1801-4 Building Grammar & Writing Skills

Name _____ Date _____

What's the Question?

Asking sentences end with a question mark. **(?)**

Read the sentences.
Then put a question mark after each question.

1. Are you cold

2. Is that your dog

3. Sit down

4. Olivia likes chocolate cake

5. Who said that

6. What is your name

7. Maria is very smart

8. Why is the light on

Sentences that begin with the asking words **who**, **what**, **when**, **where**, **why**, and **how** usually end with a question mark. Make up your own asking questions. Remember to end each one with a question mark.

Who _____

What _____

When _____

Where _____

Why _____

How _____

0-7424-1801-4 Building Grammar & Writing Skills

Name _____ Date _____

What a Surprise!

Use an exclamation point (**!**) to show surprise or strong feelings.

Read each sentence.
Ask yourself if it shows surprise or strong feelings. If it does, put an exclamation point at the end.

1. I can't believe we won

2. Oh, no

3. It's very cold today

4. Wow, I can't believe it

5. Hooray

6. Watch out

7. This sweater is warm

8. I don't like that book

9. Be careful

10. Ouch

0-7424-1801-4 Building Grammar & Writing Skills

Name _____ Date _____

Quote Me

Use quotation marks (" ") around the exact words someone says.

Example: "I like cookies," said Justin.

Read the sentences.
Put quotation marks around the words the person said.
Hint: Periods, commas, questions marks, and exclamation points go inside quotation marks.

1. Eric asked, What do you want for your birthday?

2. I want a new baseball bat, Morgan answered.

3. I love baseball, said Leo.

4. Emma said, I'm not surprised.

5. You play it all the time, added Grant.

6. Eric's mom asked, Who would like some juice?

7. I would, answered Leo.

8. Morgan said, So would I.

9. Come to the kitchen, Mom replied.

10. Okay, everyone said together.

0-7424-1801-4 Building Grammar & Writing Skills

Name _____ Date _____

Who Said That?

Read the story.
Underline the name of each speaker.
Then put quotation marks around the words he or she said.

Class Guest

1. Ms. Chaney said, Class, we have a guest today.
This is Officer Dan and his dog Toby.

2. Hello, class, said Officer Dan.

3. Hello, the students replied.

4. Officer Dan explained, I am a police officer.
Toby is my partner.

5. Max asked, Can we pet him?

6. Sure, said Officer Dan.

7. Woof, said Toby.

8. Did you train Toby? Bryan asked.

9. Police dogs have special trainers,
Officer Dan replied. He's a very
smart dog.

38

Name _____ Date _____

Mine and Yours

An **apostrophe** shows ownership.
Add an apostrophe and **s** to show who or what something belongs to.

Example: Jenny's kitten is soft

Underline the correct word to complete each sentence.

1. The (birds   bird's) nest is high in the tree.

2. Did you see (Ryan's   Ryans) puppy?

3. That is the (teachers   teacher's) pen.

4. I rode (Sam's   Sams) bike.

5. The (rabbits   rabbit's) ears are very long.

6. (Helens   Helen's) room is blue and white.

7. That (book's   books) cover is funny.

8. (Tanyas   Tanya's) jacket is torn.

9. The (dog's   dogs) coat is shiny.

10. Do you have (Rachel's   Rachels) notebook?

39

      0-7424-1801-4 Building Grammar & Writing Skills

Name _____ Date _____

Starry Nouns

A **noun** names a person, place, or thing.

Examples: bird, girl, school

Look at the words in the stars. Color the stars with nouns.

sock

shoe

heavy

green

plant

gift

cherry

snake

water

shell

flag

run

fast

nest

cry

horse

pool

forest

tall

river

40

0-7424-1801-4 Building Grammar & Writing Skills

Name _____ Date _____

Person, Place, or Thing?

Look at the nouns in the word box.
Write nouns that name a person under **Person**.
Write nouns that name a place under **Place**.
Write nouns that name a thing under **Thing**.

Word Box

teacher	store	snow	coat
book	park	beach	boots
school	doctor	artist	grandpa

Person

Place

Thing

_____   _____   _____

_____   _____   _____

_____   _____   _____

_____   _____   _____

_____   _____   _____

41

   0-7424-1801-4 Building Grammar & Writing Skills

Name _____ Date _____

Who Is It?

Draw a picture of a person.
Write the name of the person below your picture.
Do the same for a place and a thing.
Then write a sentence about your pictures.

Example: <u>Tyler</u> rode his <u>bike</u> to <u>school</u>.

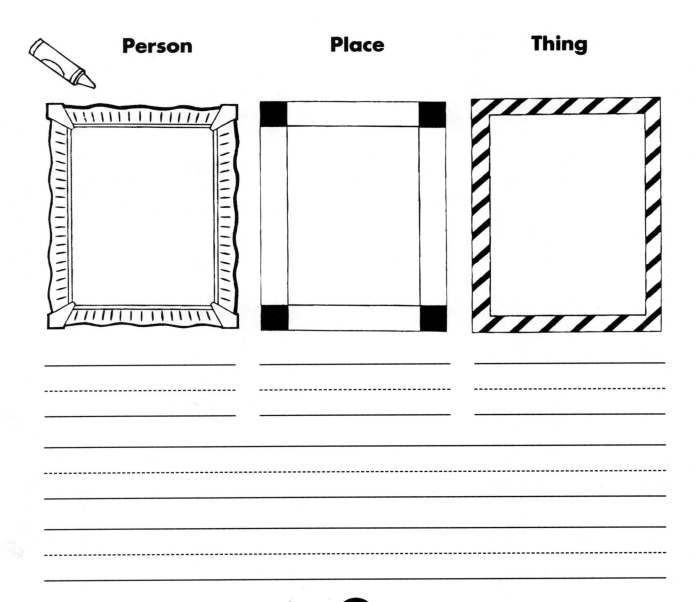

Person   **Place**   **Thing**

_____ _____ _____
- - - - - - - - - - - - - - - - - - - - - - - - - - -
_____ _____ _____

_____
- -
_____
- -
_____

42

Name _____ Date _____

Practice with Nouns

Underline the nouns in each sentence.
Hint: There may be more than one, or none!

1. Jeremy ate a sandwich.

2. The rabbit is brown and white.

3. Stop!

4. Where is your pencil?

5. Roland is seven years old.

6. Put the book away.

7. You won the game!

8. The fish swam around the pond.

9. Rosie was born in Kansas.

10. The wind blew the door open.

Name _____ Date _____

Zoo View

Read these zoo signs for each animal.
Underline the nouns.

The lion is a large cat.

It eats meat. A lion family

is called a pride.

Lion babies are called cubs.

A giraffe is a mammal.

It is the tallest land

mammal.

It eats plants.

The giraffe has long legs.

A crocodile is a

large reptile.

It lives and hunts in water.

It eats meat.

A crocodile lays eggs.

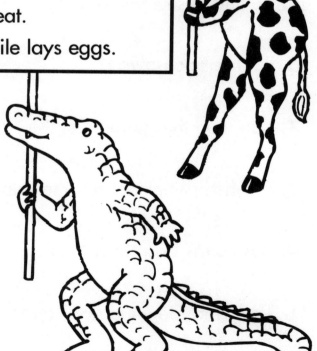

44

Name _____ Date _____

Perfectly Proper

Names of specific people, places, and things are called **proper nouns**. Proper nouns begin with a capital letter.

Examples:

Common Nouns	**Proper Nouns**
teacher	Mrs. Jones
park	Wild Oak Park
street	First Street

Draw a line from the common noun on the left to its name (proper noun) on the right.

dessert	Valentine's Day
country	The Cat in the Hat
car	Cinderella
holiday	Frosty Yum Ice Cream
road	Ford
state	Green Road
song	"Happy Birthday"
movie	England
book	California

Name _____ Date _____

More Than One

A **plural noun** tells about more than one person, place, or thing.
To make most nouns plural, you add an **s** at the end.

Examples: hat + s = hats
book + s = books

Add an **s** to each noun to make it plural.
Write the new word on the line.

1. bird _____

2. kitten _____

3. tree _____

4. glove _____

5. crayon _____

6. egg _____

7. car _____

8. picture _____

9. star _____

10. truck _____

46

Name _____ Date _____

More Plurals

If a noun ends in s, ss, sh, ch, or x, add **es** to make it plural.

Examples: bus   buses
class   classes
bush   bushes
peach peaches
box   boxes

Underline the letter or letters at the end of each word that tell you how to make the plural. Write the plural nouns on the lines. The first one is done for you.

1. glass glasses

2. match

3. gas

4. watch

5. tax

6. brush

7. switch

8. dress

9. wish

10. mix

0-7424-1801-4 Building Grammar & Writing Skills

Name _____ Date _____

Making Plurals

Look at the pictures. Add an **s** or **es** to make each noun plural.

shoe -------- _____   kiss -------- _____   fox -------- _____   lunch -------- _____

shell -------- _____   dish -------- _____   church -------- _____   box -------- _____

pot -------- _____   patch -------- _____   chair -------- _____   clock -------- _____

48

   0-7424-1801-4 Building Grammar & Writing Skills

Name _____ Date _____

All About Action

Verbs are action words. They tell what is happening in a sentence.
Example: Corey **jumps** over the fence.

Underline the action word in each sentence.

1. She hides under the bed.

2. We eat pizza for lunch.

3. I swim on a team

4. The bunny hops.

5. Gina dances at school.

6. You laugh at everything!

7. Throw your trash in the bin.

8. Emilio swings higher than his brother.

9. I ride my horse every day.

10. Draw a picture of your favorite food.

0-7424-1801-4 Building Grammar & Writing Skills

Name _____ Date _____

A Day at the Beach

Look at the picture.
Use action words from the picture to complete the sentences below.

_____

1. Doug and Staci _____ in the sand.

2. Wade can _____ a sandcastle.

3. Emily _____ with her puppy.

4. Mom will _____ a drink for me.

5. Maddie _____ her ice-cream cone.

6. Drew _____ in the ocean.

50

   0-7424-1801-4 Building Grammar & Writing Skills

Name _____ Date _____

Word Match

Nouns and verbs work together in sentences. If the noun tells about one person, place, or thing, the verb has an **s** at the end. If the noun is plural, there is no **s** at the end.

Example: they <u>run</u>
he <u>runs</u>

Underline the correct verb that completes each sentence.

1. John (play   plays) the piano.

2. Beverly (want   wants) to go with us.

3. The horses (eat   eats) hay.

4. Mae (bake   bakes) cookies.

5. They (like   likes) chocolate ice cream.

6. The dog (bark   barks) at the door.

7. The rain (hit   hits) the window.

8. The team (wears   wear) red jackets.

9. Cindy never (drink   drinks) soda.

10. Her parents (plant   plants) a garden.

0-7424-1801-4 Building Grammar & Writing Skills

Name _____ Date _____

Now and Then

Some verbs tell about actions happening now. Some tell about actions that happened in the past. These are called **past-tense verbs**.

Add **ed** to make most verbs past tense.
If the word already ends in **e** just add **d**.

Example: walk = action now
walk**ed** = past action

Read the sentences.
Write **P** if the verb
tells about the past.
Write **N** if the verb tells
what is happening now.

1. Judy and her sister walk to school. _____

2. Regina walked to her friend's house. _____

3. Kent watched the parade. _____

4. Miguel rides his horse after school. _____

5. Kerry loved her lost kitten. _____

Add **d** or **ed** to make these verbs past tense.

live _____   help _____   look _____   talk _____   close _____

52

Name _____ Date _____

Being Now

Is, **am**, and **are** belong to the "to be" family of verbs. They tell about "being" something now.

Example: John **is** thirsty.
I **am** thirsty.
They **are** thirsty.

Read the sentences.
Underline the "being" verb.
Draw a line to match the sentence to the correct picture.

1. Jennifer is happy.

2. Rich is wet.

3. Devon and Todd are asleep.

4. It is raining.

5. Britney is sad.

6. She is wearing a baseball cap.

7. The lions are roaring.

8. I am tired.

0-7424-1801-4 Building Grammar & Writing Skills

Name _____ Date _____

Being in the Past

Was and **were** are also members of the "to be" verb family. They tell about "being" in the past.

Example: She **was**
You **were**
They **were**

Underline the correct verb that completes each sentence.

1. I (was   were) there yesterday.

2. You (was   were) working hard.

3. He (was   were) afraid of spiders.

4. It (was   were) very cold last week.

5. They (was   were) riding in the car.

6. Scott (was   were) on his skateboard.

7. Yesterday we (was   were) in Arizona.

8. Today we (was   were) in New Mexico.

9. My sister (was   were) a hockey player.

10. My dad and uncle (was   were) football players.

   0-7424-1801-4 Building Grammar & Writing Skills

Name _____ Date _____

Ready for Review

Remember, **nouns** name a person, place, or thing. **Verbs** are action words.

Color the birds with verbs **blue**. Color the birds with nouns **red**.

0-7424-1801-4 Building Grammar & Writing Skills

Name _____ Date _____

Pronoun Power

Pronouns take the place of nouns.

Examples: <u>**Andy**</u> wrote a letter.   My <u>**rat**</u> is smart.
<u>**He**</u> wrote a letter.   <u>**It**</u> is smart.

Pronouns

I	we	he	she	it	they
me	us	him	her	you	them

Read the sentences.
Replace the underlined noun or nouns with a pronoun from the box.

1. <u>Tara and I</u> went to the park.

---------------------- went to the park.
_____

2. <u>William</u> liked <u>the play</u>.

---------------------- liked ----------------------
_____   _____ .

3. <u>Tana and Joe</u> are reading.

---------------------- are reading.
_____

4. Randy gave <u>the book</u> to <u>Sara</u>.

Randy gave ---------------------- to ----------------------
_____   _____ .

5. <u>Becka</u> dropped her doll.

----------------------dropped her doll.
_____

56

    0-7424-1801-4 Building Grammar & Writing Skills

Name _____ Date _____

Me, Oh My!

I and **me** are pronouns. Use **I** and **me** when you talk about yourself. Use **I** when you are doing the action. Use **me** when you are receiving the action.

Example: **I** learn.
My teacher showed **me**.

Read the sentences.
Circle words that are doing the action.
Underline words that are receiving action.

1. I gave Leslie my cookie.

2. Leslie gave her carrot sticks to me.

3. I will go to the mall with my dad and my sister.

4. My sister will go to the mall with me.

5. Grapes are good for me.

6. I am writing a letter.

7. Write a sentence using the word **I**.

_____

- -

_____

8. Write a sentence using the word **me**.

_____

- -

_____

 0-7424-1801-4 Building Grammar & Writing Skills

Name _____ Date _____

Describing Words

Adjectives are words that describe nouns.

Look at the pictures and read the adjectives.
Circle the adjectives that describe the picture.

1.		crackling	icy	hot
2.		wet	soft	cozy
3.		sharp	floppy	pointed
4.		brave	happy	slimy
5.		wet	soapy	flat
6.		fuzzy	spotted	small
7.		noisy	tired	drowsy
8.		crunchy	sweet	square

0-7424-1801-4 Building Grammar & Writing Skills

Name _____ Date _____

Sizes and Shapes

Some **adjectives** tell about size and shape.
Choose an adjective from the word box.
Write it on the line.
Draw a picture of something that the adjective describes.

Word Box

big	heavy	tall	round
square	long	short	tiny

_____

- - - - - - - - - - - - - - - - - - -

_____

Pick an adjective from the word box to complete each sentence.

1. The basketball player is _____ .

2. The elephant is _____ .

3. This coin is _____ .

4. That snake is _____ .

5. Those boxes are _____ .

59

   0-7424-1801-4 Building Grammar & Writing Skills

Name _____ Date _____

Colors and Numbers

Colors and numbers are describing words.
Pick a number or color from the word box to describe each picture.

Word Box

black	green	red	white	yellow
one	two	three	four	

_____

- - - - - - -

_____

_____

- - - - - - -

_____

_____

- - - - - - -

_____

0-7424-1801-4 Building Grammar & Writing Skills

Name _____ Date _____

Picture This

Pick two **adjectives** from the word box that describe each picture.
Write them on the lines.
Hint: You can use words more than once.

Word Box

big	square	tall	icy	gray
white	fast	exciting	happy	sweet
long	cold	warm	heavy	cozy

Name _____ Date _____

Comparing Things

Some **adjectives** compare things. When you compare two things, add **er** to the adjective.

Example: Jacki is **taller** than Kim.

When you compare more than two things, add **est** to the adjective.

Example: Jacki is the **tallest** in her class.

Read the sentences. Add an **er** or **est** after each adjective.

1. Brandon is tall ------------- than his brother.

2. This is the long ------------- snake in the zoo.

3. It is the bright ------------- star in the sky.

4. Your cookie is small ------------- than mine.

5. Maile is the smart ------------- in her family.

6. That blue bounces high ------------- than the red ball.

62

   0-7424-1801-4 Building Grammar & Writing Skills

Name _____ Date _____

Adverb Trees

An **adverb** describes a verb. An adverb tells when, where, or how something happened.

Examples: She walks **quickly**. (how)
She walks **early** in the morning. (when)
She walks **over** the bridge. (where)

Look at the adverbs in the word box.
Decide if each adverb tells how, when, or where.
Then write it under the correct word.

Word Box

under	softly	here	away
weekly	carefully	loudly	later
slowly	yesterday	often	nearby

When	**Where**	**How**
_____	_____	_____
_____	_____	_____
_____	_____	_____
_____	_____	_____
_____	_____	_____

Name _____ Date _____

Ready for Review

Read the sentences.
Underline the adjectives in green.
Underline the adverbs in red.

1. Grandma has a beautiful hat with pink ribbons.

2. The big, blue car drove by slowly.

3. I will read the book later.

4. Rebecca lives here.

5. The party started late.

6. The baby cried loudly.

7. The two happy dogs played outside.

8. Sometimes Cassie walks nearby.

9. Danny rode his red bike in the race.

10. The nice gardener arrives weekly.

0-7424-1801-4 Building Grammar & Writing Skills

Name _____ Date _____

I'd Like to Introduce . . .

The words **a** and **an** are called **articles**. They "introduce" nouns. **A** introduces a noun that starts with a consonant. **An** usually introduces a noun that starts with a vowel.

Examples: Theo bought **a** hamburger.
Kelly ate **an** egg sandwich.

Write the correct article to "introduce" each noun.

_____ cat

_____ egg

_____ bike

_____ eye

_____ fox

_____ oar

_____ book

_____ ax

_____ fish

_____ daisy

_____ ant

_____ umbrella

65

Name _____ Date _____

More Introductions

The is an **article**. **The** "introduces" a specific thing or things.
Example: The coat is mine.
Write **the**, **a**, or **an** to complete each sentence.

1. _____ big, brown horse is very fast.

2. I saw a picture of _____ horse.

3. A fox is _____ animal.

4. _____ blue umbrella is mine.

5. Cleo draws with _____ orange crayon

6. George is _____ class president.

7. My baby brother took _____ nap.

8. _____ new puppy chewed on _____ bone.

9. The teacher spoke to _____ principal.

10. Today is _____ sunny day.

0-7424-1801-4 Building Grammar & Writing Skills

Name _____ Date _____

Creating Compounds

Sometimes you can put two words together to make a new word.
The new word is called a **compound word**.

Read the words below.
Then draw a line to match two words that make a compound word.
The first one is done for you.

1. bed		light
2. finger		nail
3. water		box
4. air		house
5. hall		way
6. rain		room
7. sand		drop
8. dog		fall
9. some		plane
10. sun		body

BISCUIT

© McGraw-Hill Children's Publishing 0-7424-1801-4 Building Grammar & Writing Skills

Name _____ Date _____

Two Makes One

Pick one word from **List #1** and **List #2** to make a compound word. Write your new word by the matching picture.

List #1	**List #2**
water	pot
rain	stairs
door	house
light	walk
up	bird
pan	ball
side	cake
basket	melon
flower	knob
blue	coat

0-7424-1801-4 Building Grammar & Writing Skills

Name _____ Date _____

Synonym Search

Synonyms are words with the same or almost the same meaning.

Example: happy=cheery, glad, joyful.

Draw a line to match the words with the same or almost the same meaning.

1. neat		furry
2. cold		breeze
3. wind		angry
4. kind		woof
5. plate		tidy
6. small		blossom
7. fluffy		chilly
8. mad		little
9. bark		dish
10. flower		nice

69

Name _____ Date _____

Tangled Words

Use a different color crayon to trace each balloon string.
You will find word pairs with the same meaning.
Then color each pair of balloons a different color.

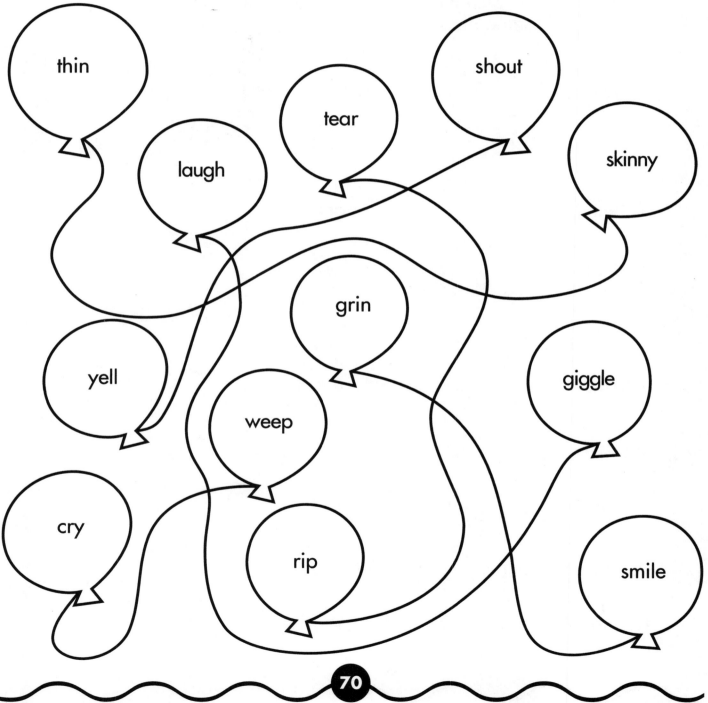

0-7424-1801-4 Building Grammar & Writing Skills

Name _____ Date _____

Silly Sentences

Antonyms are words that have opposite meanings.

Examples: hot=cold
sweet=sour
dark=light

Read each underlined word.
Then circle its antonym at the end of the sentence.

1. The puddle made Courtney's feet <u>wet</u>. (itchy   dry)

2. Paul was <u>fast</u> enough to win the race. (dirty   slow)

3. Dad climbed up the <u>tall</u> ladder.   (short   blue)

4. The glass was <u>full</u> of cold milk.   (empty   cold)

5. Caroline slid <u>down</u> the slide.   (over   up)

6. Most people sleep at <u>night</u>. (day   sunrise)

7. The book is on the <u>top</u> shelf. (bottom   tall)

8. <u>Close</u> the box and put it away. (stop   open)

9. The <u>tiny</u> kitten drank the milk.   (furry   huge)

10. The <u>love</u> chocolate cake! (hate   like)

0-7424-1801-4 Building Grammar & Writing Skills

Name _____ Date _____

Opposites Puzzle

Find the opposite of each word below in the word box.
Then write the word from the box in the puzzle.

ACROSS

2. lost

3. large

4. wide

5. day

8. mean

DOWN

1. smile

3. happy

6. light

7. hard

9. far

Word Box	
dark	frown
sad	near
kind	found
soft	night
narrow	small

0-7424-1801-4 Building Grammar & Writing Skills

Name _____ Date _____

Sound-Alikes

Examples: hear, here
I, eye
sea, see

Some words sound alike, but they have different meanings.
Read the sentence pairs.
Underline the two words that sound alike.

1. Brooke has red hair.
A hare has very long ears.

2. The teacher will meet
my parents.
I love meat and potatoes.

3. Choose the right word.
I can write the alphabet.

4. The wind blew all day.
Brianne has blue eyes.

5. Lita has two pencils.
I want to go too

6. The apple is red.
Mom read the book aloud.

7. There was one cookie left.
Eddie won the race.

8. The puppy liked her new toy.
Kaitlyn knew the answer.

9. The bee buzzed around
the flower.
I want to be a firefighter.

10. Alexis ate a piece of cake.
Josh is eight years old.

0-7424-1801-4 Building Grammar & Writing Skills

Name _____ Date _____

Matching Sounds

Read each word.
Then draw a line to match the word and picture that sound alike.

1. so

2. knows

3. pair

4. son

5. stares

6. not

7. to

8. I

9. rode

10. would

0-7424-1801-4 Building Grammar & Writing Skills

Name _____ Date _____

Listen Up!

Some words describe a sound. Some words even "sound" like the sound they're describing!

Look at the pictures.
Choose a word from the word box that describes the sound each makes. Write the words.

Word Box

meow	tweet	ring
boom	splat	tick-tock

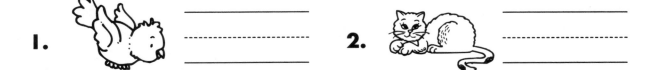

1. _____

2. _____

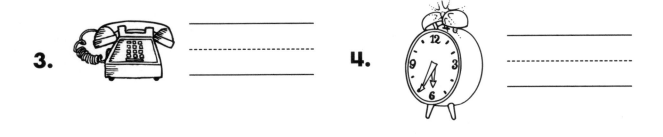

3. _____

4. _____

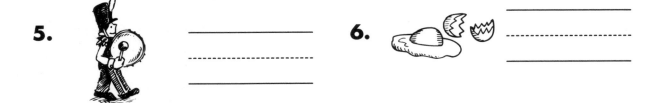

5. _____

6. _____

Name _____ Date _____

It Sounds Like . . .

Read the sound word by each box.
Draw a picture to go with it.

crash	**quack**	**drip**	**honk**

Make up your own sound words.
Draw a picture to go with each word.

_____

_____

0-7424-1801-4 Building Grammar & Writing Skills

Name _____ Date _____

Rhyme Time

Rhyming words end with the same sound.

Examples: top   pop
fly   cry
ran   plan

Draw lines to connect the three words that rhyme.
The first one is done for you.

1. wing	sea	sing
2. cold	sold	wheel
3. mouse	sock	jet
4. block	king	gold
5. meal	seal	tea
6. tree	house	wood
7. bank	wet	blank
8. pet	new	blouse
9. blue	hood	two
10. good	tank	clock

0-7424-1801-4 Building Grammar & Writing Skills

Name _____ Date _____

Making Contractions

A **contraction** is two words put together, but some letters are left out. An **apostrophe** takes the place of the missing letters.

Examples: can not   can ~~not~~   can't
          she is   she ~~is~~   she's
          you will   you ~~will~~   you'll
          they are   they ~~are~~   they're

Write the number on the line to match each set of words to its contraction.

1. he is   _____ she'll

2. it is   _____ I'll

3. you are   _____ we're

4. we are   _____ he's

5. I am   _____ aren't

6. I will   _____ don't

7. she will   _____ you're

8. would not   _____ it's

9. do not   _____ I'm

10. are not   _____ wouldn't

78

0-7424-1801-4 Building Grammar & Writing Skills

Name _____ Date _____

Team Up

Read the sentences.
Use the words under the lines to write a contraction to complete each sentence.

Example: Kristin **won't** be running today.
         (will not)

1. Byron and Jamie ---------------------- going to run the race.
                     (are not)

2. ---------------------- too cold outside.
   (It is)

3. Ramona ---------------------- run without her lucky shoes.
             (will not)

4. ---------------------- the fastest runner on the team.
   (She is)

5. ---------------------- see Logan at the track meet.
   (You will)

6. Ryan says ---------------------- going to win.
            (he is)

7. Ramona ---------------------- find her lucky shoes!
         (can not)

8. ---------------------- going to pass out drinks to the runners.
   (I am)

       0-7424-1801-4 Building Grammar & Writing Skills

Name _____ Date _____

Simple Subjects

The **naming part** (subject) of a sentence tells who or what the sentence is about.

Example: <u>My aunt</u> baked cookies.

Read the sentences.
Underline the naming part of each sentence.

1. I live on River Street.

2. The school band played well.

3. The zoo is open today.

4. The yellow bird sang.

5. Snow and ice covered the road.

6. Angela likes to swim.

7. Andrew's boots are too tight.

8. Claire's bike has a pink basket.

9. A cold wind blew the leaves away.

10. The girls on the soccer team ran fast.

0-7424-1801-4 Building Grammar & Writing Skills

Name _____ Date _____

It's All in the Action

The **action part** (predicate) of a sentence tells what happened.
Example: My aunt **baked cookies**.

Underline the action part of each sentence.

1. My pet rabbit eats bananas.

2. Linda brushed her long hair.

3. The teacher wrote on the board.

4. She threw candy into the crowd.

5. George kicked the ball.

6. That sweater is pretty.

7. The artist painted a picture of clouds.

8. The vase broke when it fell.

9. It snowed all night.

10. The ball bounced down the stairs.

81

Name _____ Date _____

Complete Sentences

A **complete sentence** begins with a capital letter. It has a naming part (subject) and an action part (predicate).

These sentence parts are mixed up. Draw a line to match the naming part of each sentence to the action part.

1. My favorite shirt   fly south for the winter.

2. The kitten   is blue.

3. My horse   won the baking contest.

4. I   has striped fur.

5. Some birds   gallops very fast.

Rewrite each sentence below:

1. _____

2. _____

3. _____

4. _____

5. _____

82

Name _____ Date _____

It's Not Finished

Some of these sentences are incomplete.
Write **N** next to those missing the naming part.
Write **A** next to those missing the action part.

1. The silly clown

2. Susan and her sister

3. went to the water park

4. ran all the way home

5. My uncle with red hair

6. likes the lions

7. The man next door

8. waits for me

9. My friend who likes horses

10. The woman in the blue dress

Name _____ Date _____

Crack the Code

Use the secret code to put these sentences together.
Each number stands for a letter.
Write the letter above the matching number below.
Two of the sentences are incomplete.
Circle them.

Secret Code

a	b	c	d	e	f	g	h	i	j	k	l	m
1	2	3	4	5	6	7	8	9	10	11	12	13
n	o	p	q	r	s	t	u	v	w	x	y	z
14	15	16	17	18	19	20	21	22	23	24	25	26

1. __ __   __ __ __ __ __ __   __ __ __ __ .
    13 25   6 18 9 5 14 4   10 1 3 11

2. __ __ __   __ __   __ __ __ __ __ .
    12 1 14   9 19   8 1 16 16 25

3. __ __ __ __   __ __ __ __ __   __ __ __ .
    2 9 12 12   12 9 11 5 19   16 9 5

4. __   __ __ __   __ __ __ __ __   __ __ __ __ .
    9   18 1 14   20 15 20 8 5   16 1 18 11

5. __ __ __   __ __ __ __ __   __ __ __ .
    20 8 5   2 12 1 3 11   4 15 7

0-7424-1801-4 Building Grammar & Writing Skills

Name _____ Date _____

Tell All About It

A **telling sentence** explains something. It begins with a capital letter and ends with a period. **(.)**

Read the sentences.
Circle letters that should be capitals.
Put a period at the end of each sentence.

1. robyn went to the basketball game

2. i am thirsty

3. the room is too cold

4. my brother danny likes pizza

5. roger ran to school

6. the boy wrote his name on the board

7. the movie was funny

8. paul is a good artist

Write your own telling sentence. Make sure to begin with a capital letter and end with a period.

_____

- -

_____
- -
_____

85

0-7424-1801-4 Building Grammar & Writing Skills

Name _____ Date _____

I'm Asking

An **asking sentence** asks a question. It begins with a capital letter and ends with a question mark. **(?)**

Find the asking sentences in the puzzle.
Write a question mark after each one.
Then color the spaces that have asking sentences.

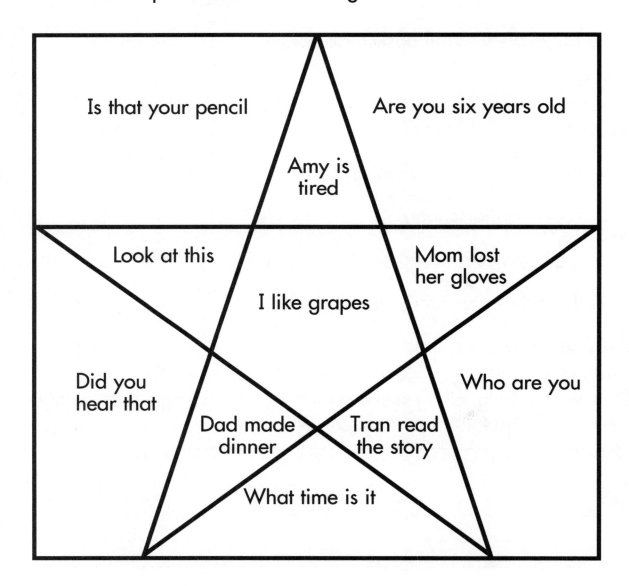

Is that your pencil

Are you six years old

Amy is tired

Look at this

Mom lost her gloves

I like grapes

Did you hear that

Who are you

Dad made dinner

Tran read the story

What time is it

0-7424-1801-4 Building Grammar & Writing Skills

Name _____ Date _____

Telling or Asking

Read the sentences.
Put a period at the end of the telling sentences.
Put a question mark at the end of the asking sentences.

1. The teddy bear has a big bow

2. I am six years old

3. How old are you

4. My book is blue

5. Is that your book

6. John has a puppy

7. Do you want to play

8. Did James do his homework

9. It is raining

10. Can you run fast

0-7424-1801-4 Building Grammar & Writing Skills

Name _____   Date _____

Make a Change

You can change a telling sentence into an asking sentence. Just change the order of the words.

Examples: You are ready.
Are you ready?

Change each telling sentence into an asking sentence. The first one is done for you.

1. The balloon is red.
<u>Is the balloon red?</u>

2. You do like pizza. _____

_____

3. He does want to run. _____

_____

4. My book is here. _____

_____

5. She will write the letter. _____

_____

6. The cat is striped. _____

_____

88

Name _____ Date _____

Mix and Match

Write your own sentences!
Choose one word from each box to make each sentence.

John	runs	fast
I	walk	home
you	sleep	nicely
we	eats	alone
Helen	look	late
Grandma	tell	notes
Mrs. Tucker	writes	secrets
teacher	likes	jokes

1. John likes to write notes.

_____

2. _____

_____

3. _____

_____

4. _____

_____

5. _____

0-7424-1801-4 Building Grammar & Writing Skills

Name _____ Date _____

Word Scramble

These words are in the wrong order.
Write the words in order to make a sentence.
Put a period, question mark, or exclamation point at the end.
Start the first word with a capital letter.

1. long horses legs have

_____

_____

2. the shining stars are

_____

_____

3. peanut I butter like

_____

_____

4. won first I prize

_____

_____

5. gate closed is the

_____

_____

6. sam mike are and friends

_____

_____

Name _____ Date _____

What's the Idea?

The **main idea** tells what something is about.
Look at the picture.
Then underline the main idea.

The boy likes rides.

Lambs are baby sheep.

The children are feeding the animals.

Cotton candy is tasty.

0-7424-1801-4 Building Grammar & Writing Skills

Name _____ Date _____

The Main Idea

Read each story.
Underline the main idea.

1. Jordan's family is building a swimming pool. Jordan wants to learn to swim. His best friend, Jose, is going to help. Jose's brother teaches swimming. Jordan can't wait to get started.

2. The bunny wanted to eat carrots. She crept into Mrs. Mason's garden. She nibbled on a carrot. Mrs. Mason shooed her away. Bunny will try again tomorrow.

3. Beverly was a clown for Halloween. She wore a red wig. She had a big red nose. Beverly had so much fun. She may be a clown next Halloween, too!

© McGraw-Hill Children's Publishing 0-7424-1801-4 Building Grammar & Writing Skills

Name _____ Date _____

Patrick's Present

Stories are written in order.
The sentences in this story are all mixed up! Write the numbers **1** to **6**
to put them in order.
Rewrite the story below.

_____ He ran to the living room.

_____ Patrick woke up on his birthday.

_____ The card said, "Love, Mom and Dad."

_____ Patrick thanked his mom and dad with a hug.

_____ He jumped out of bed.

_____ He found a new bike with a big red ribbon.

_____

_____

_____

_____

_____

_____

_____

_____

   0-7424-1801-4 Building Grammar & Writing Skills

Name _____ Date _____

Lining Up

Andra, Trevor, Raul, and Ashley are waiting in line for ice cream.
Look at the picture.
Then follow the instructions.

1. Color **blue** the shirt of the first child in line.

2. Color **green** the shirt of the second child in line.

3. Color **yellow** the shirt of the third child in line.

4. Color **red** the shirt of the last child in line.

Write **first**, **second**, **third**, and **last** to tell in which order the
children are standing in line.

_____

1. Andra has braids.   Andra is _____.

2. Raul is wearing a blue shirt.   Raul is _____.

3. Ashley brought her dog.   Ashley is _____.

4. Trevor is holding his mitt.   Trevor is _____.

94

   0-7424-1801-4 Building Grammar & Writing Skills

Name _____ Date _____

Costume Party

Katie, Robyn, and Anna are getting ready for a costume party. Their costumes are all mixed up. Katie is going as a ballerina. Write **K** on her things. Robyn is a cowgirl. Write **R** on her things. Anna is a kitten. Write **A** on her things.

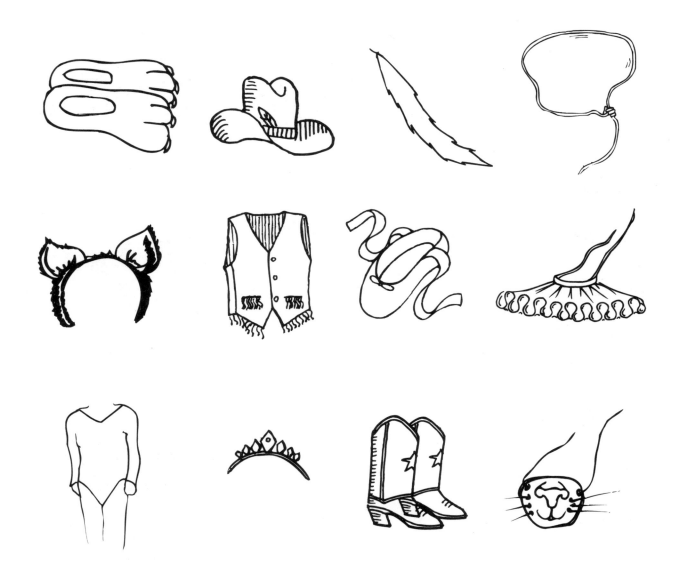

0-7424-1801-4 Building Grammar & Writing Skills

Name _____ Date _____

Finding Groups

Look at the picture.
Group the things that go together.
Color the animals yellow.
Color the plants green.
Color the toys red.

0-7424-1801-4 Building Grammar & Writing Skills

Name _____ Date _____

What Doesn't Belong?

Look at each row of objects.
Cross out the object in each row that does not belong.

1.

2.

3.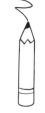

4.

5.

0-7424-1801-4 Building Grammar & Writing Skills

Name _____ Date _____

Ringed Seals

A **paragraph** is made up of sentences. The sentences are about one main idea.

Read the sentences.
Circle each sentence that might be in a paragraph about the ringed seal.

1. There is a lot of ice at the North Pole.

2. The ringed seal is five feet long.

3. It lives in the Arctic.

4. Many animals know how to swim.

5. I can swim.

6. The ringed seal eats fish.

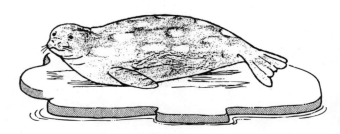

7. It is a very good swimmer.

8. Some whales eat fish.

9. The ringed seal is a sea mammal.

10. Sea lions have long flippers.

0-7424-1801-4 Building Grammar & Writing Skills

Name _____ Date _____

Movie Mania

Read the paragraph.
Circle the words that make the paragraph about what you like!

I like to go to the movies. My (parents friends grandparents) go with me. I like (funny scary action) movies the best. My favorite movie snack is (popcorn candy hot dogs). I wish I could go to the movies (two five ten) times a month!

Rewrite your paragraph below:

_____

_____

_____

_____

_____

_____

0-7424-1801-4 Building Grammar & Writing Skills

Name _____ Date _____

In the End

Every **paragraph** has an ending sentence. It usually "sums up" the idea in the paragraph.

Read each paragraph.
Then pick the best ending sentence.
Write it on the line.

My Puppy, Barney

One day I found a puppy. I looked for the owner. My dad helped me put up signs. No one came to get the puppy. So, my mom said we could keep him.

1. My friend Ted has a cat.
2. A also have fish.
3. I named my puppy Barney.
4. Dogs like to bark.

_____

I Love Baseball

Baseball is my favorite sport. I play first base on my baseball team. I am also a pretty good hitter. My team plays every summer, but I wish we played all year round.

1. I want to play catcher.
2. I like soccer too.
3. My dad used to play baseball.
4. I could play baseball every day.

_____

0-7424-1801-4 Building Grammar & Writing Skills

Name _____ Date _____

Scrambled Sentences

This paragraph is all mixed up!
Put these scrambled sentences in order
to make a beginning, middle, and end.
Number the sentences **1** to **9**.

_____
_____ But we didn't catch anything.
_____

_____ We packed warm clothes and sleeping bags.
_____

_____ I would like to go camping again.
_____

_____ Then we went fishing.
_____
_____

_____ We drove to Lake Serenity.
_____

_____ The next day was sunny, and we went home.
_____

_____ When we got to the lake, we put up our tent.
_____

_____ We went camping last week.
_____
_____

_____ It started to rain, so we went to bed early.
_____

101

        0-7424-1801-4 Building Grammar & Writing Skills

Name _____ Date _____

Fact Find

Kendra is writing a report about snakes.
Read her paragraph.
Then write **T** for **true** or **F** for **false** on the lines.

Snakes

Snakes are reptiles. They do not have legs or ears. Snakes have scales. They shed their skin. Some snakes have venom. They kill their prey with a bite. Some snakes squeeze their prey. Most snakes lay eggs. The largest snakes can be 20 feet long.

1. _____ Snakes are reptiles.

2. _____ All snakes are green.

3. _____ Snakes shed their skin.

4. _____ Some snakes kill prey with a bite.

5. _____ Some snakes kill prey with sharp spikes.

6. _____ Snakes never swim.

7. _____ Snakes drink milk.

8. _____ Most snakes lay eggs.

9. _____ Snakes have scales.

10. _____ Some snakes have small legs.

0-7424-1801-4 Building Grammar & Writing Skills

Name _____ Date _____

Organize an Outline

An **outline** can help you put your ideas in order. Look at the titles in the outline. Write the words from the word box under the correct subjects.

Word Box

dog	cow	tiger
polar bear	elephant	chicken
goldfish	horse	canary

Animals

1. Pets

A. _____ B. _____ C. _____

2. Wild animals

A. _____ B. _____ C. _____

3. Farm animals

A. _____ B. _____ C. _____

0-7424-1801-4 Building Grammar & Writing Skills

Name _____ Date _____

All About Insects

Read the sentences in the puzzle.
Decide which ones should go in a paragraph about insects.
Color these shapes to find out who's hiding!

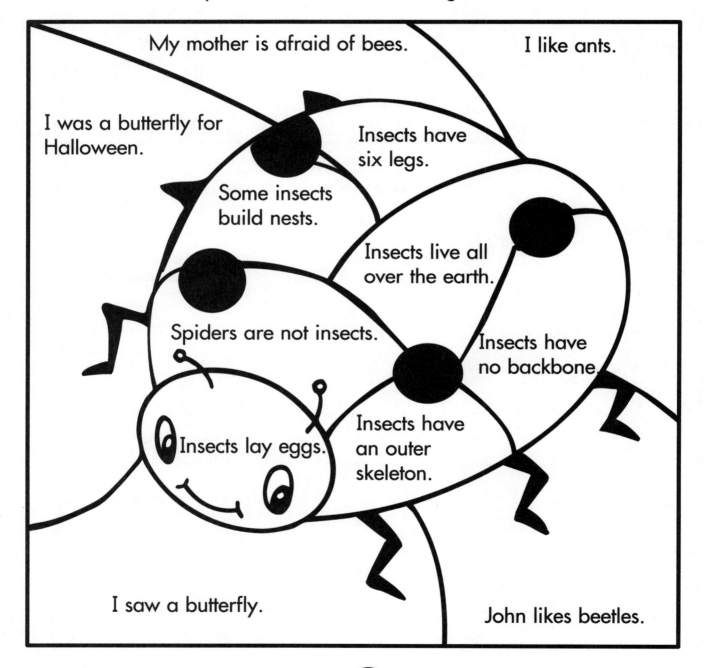

My mother is afraid of bees.

I like ants.

I was a butterfly for Halloween.

Insects have six legs.

Some insects build nests.

Insects live all over the earth.

Spiders are not insects.

Insects have no backbone.

Insects lay eggs.

Insects have an outer skeleton.

I saw a butterfly.

John likes beetles.

104

Name _____ Date _____

Dear Friend

Wendy wrote a letter to her friend.
Use words from the word box to tell about the letter.

Word Box

date	greeting	body of letter
closing	name	

April 7, 2003

Dear Rebecca,

I had a nice time at your party. The games were fun. I hope you had a happy birthday.

Your friend,

Wendy

0-7424-1801-4 Building Grammar & Writing Skills

Name _____ Date _____

Thank You!

Do you know someone who deserves a "thank you"?
Write a thank-you note to that person.
You can use the ideas below.

1. Thank you for the nice gift.
2. Thank you for being so nice.
3. Thank you for thinking of me.

Date _____

Dear _____,

_____

_____

_____

_____

_____

Your friend,

_____

0-7424-1801-4 Building Grammar & Writing Skills

Name _____ Date _____

My Story

Some people write stories about their own lives. You can too!

Fill in the lines below, and you will have a story about you!
Finish your story by drawing your picture in the frame.

_____

My name is _____ .

My favorite toy is _____ .

My favorite color is _____ .

I like to eat _____ .

My friends are _____ .

What I like about school is

_____

_____ .

_____

My favorite things to do are

_____

_____

_____

_____

_____

       0-7424-1801-4 Building Grammar & Writing Skills

Name _____ Date _____

What Do You Think?

Look at the picture. Then answer the questions below.

1. What are the children doing? _____

2. Who decides where the plants should go? _____

3. How many more holes must they dig? _____

4. Who will water the plants? _____

5. What will the plants grow? _____

0-7424-1801-4 Building Grammar & Writing Skills

Name _____ Date _____

Dear Diary

It's fun to write in a diary about what you do and what you think.
Think about what you did today.
Write or draw three things on this diary page.
Don't forget to write the date at the top of the page!

0-7424-1801-4 Building Grammar & Writing Skills

Name _____ Date _____

Write It Right

There are 10 mistakes in this paragraph.
Circle each mistake.
Then write it correctly on another paper.

jayna was invited to spend the night at Maria s house.

she packed her toothbrush. Jayna took her favorite doll maria

was waiting for her when her mom dropped her off "Be a

good girl, her mom said. She kissed Jayna good-bye. Maria

said, I am so glad you're here!" The girls ate pizza. they

played games. Then they went to sleep. Jayna s mom picked

her up the next morning. "I will invite Maria to our house next

week," Jayna told her mom.

0-7424-1801-4 Building Grammar & Writing Skills

Name _____ Date _____

And Then . . .

Taylor made a story map for the story he's writing. A **story map** is like an outline.

Taylor's notes are all mixed up!
Number his notes from **1** to **7** to put them in order.

_____ First she jumped up and down in the nest.

_____ Cleo felt herself rising.

_____ She was high above the nest.

_____ Cleo was flying!

_____ Cleo was a very small bird.

_____ Then she opened her wings and flapped.

_____ She wanted to fly.

Now, write your own story map about what happens to Cleo next.

1. _____

2. _____

3. _____

4. _____

5. _____

0-7424-1801-4 Building Grammar & Writing Skills

Name _____ Date _____

Imagine Who

Characters are the people or animals in a story.
Draw a picture of a character you would like to tell a story about.
Then answer the questions about your character.

1. What is your character's name?

_____

- -

_____

2. What does he or she look like?

_____

- -

_____

3. What are your character's favorite things to do?

_____

- -

_____

4. What makes your character happy?

_____

- -

_____

5. What makes your character sad or scared?

_____

- -

_____

0-7424-1801-4 Building Grammar & Writing Skills

Name _____ Date _____

Imagine Where

A **setting** is where a story takes place.

Imagine a snowy place.
Draw a picture of your "snowy setting."

Write a sentence describing your snowy setting.

_____

- -

_____

Imagine a sunny place.
Draw a picture of your "sunny setting."

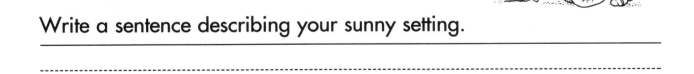

Write a sentence describing your sunny setting.

_____

- -

_____

0-7424-1801-4 Building Grammar & Writing Skills

Name _____ Date _____

Point of View

Gina, Corey, Freddie, and Rachel are writing about their school playground. They are all in the same setting, but they see different things.

Look at each picture above. Then write each child's name next to what they see.

_____

1. Today Mrs. Juarez gave out cupcakes. _____

_____

2. Today Michelle flew a kite. _____

_____

3. Today a bird built a nest. _____

_____

4. Today Ashton lost his shoe on the swings. _____

114

Name _____ Date _____

What Comes Next?

Look at the pictures.
Read the two sentences under each picture.
Then underline the sentence that tells what is going to happen next.

1. The girl with short hair will win.
2. The girl with long hair will win.

1. The glass will break.
2. The boy will catch the glass.

1. The water will not splash.
2. The water will splash the girl.

0-7424-1801-4 Building Grammar & Writing Skills

Name _____ Date _____

Telling a Story

These pictures tell a story.
Look at each picture.
Write a sentence about each one.

1. **2.** **3.** **4.** **5.**

1.
_____
- -

2.
_____
- -

3.
_____
- -

4.
_____
- -

5.
_____
- -

0-7424-1801-4 Building Grammar & Writing Skills

Name _____ Date _____

A Beautiful Walk

Sometimes you can "paint a picture" with words.
Read the story.
Circle the words that "paint" the best picture.

    Ryan went for a walk with his big sister. The day was
(cold windy cloudy). The leaves on the trees were (colorful crisp
bright). Ryan heard birds (singing chattering peeping). Ryan and
his sister walked to the bakery. Ryan smelled (cinnamon lemon
chocolate). His sister bought him a cookie. It was (warm chewy
crispy). Ryan (smiled grinned skipped) all the way home.

Now, draw a picture to go with the story.

```



```

        0-7424-1801-4 Building Grammar & Writing Skills

Name _____ Date _____

The Lost Shoe

Look at the picture.
Answer the questions.
Then write a story about the girl.

_____
_____

What is the girl's name?_____

Where is she? _____

Where is she getting ready to go?_____

Why is she worried? _____

What can she do?_____

What happens? _____

Write your story: _____

_____
_____
_____
_____
_____
_____

　　0-7424-1801-4 Building Grammar & Writing Skills

Name _____ Date _____

Animal Tale

Make up a story about an animal that no one has seen before.
Answer the questions.

1. What does your animal sound like?

_____

_____

2. What does your animal look like?

_____

3. What does it eat?

_____

4. How does it move? Does it swim, fly, walk, or crawl?

_____

Write a short paragraph about your animal:

_____

0-7424-1801-4 Building Grammar & Writing Skills

Name _____   Date _____

A Good Day

Read the beginning of the story.
Then finish it in your own words.

When I woke up this morning, I knew it would be a good day. I felt hungry. I went to the kitchen. But when I walked in I saw . . .

_____

_____

_____

_____

_____

_____

Draw a picture to go with your story:

```



```

0-7424-1801-4 Building Grammar & Writing Skills

Name _____ Date _____

Magic and Mystery

A **mystery** story makes the reader ask questions. The questions are finally answered at the end of the story.

Read the beginning of this story. Then finish it in your own words.

   Bonnie Bunny could sing like a bird. She wanted to win the school talent contest. All of the animals were practicing their acts. Tommy Tortoise was working on his juggling act. Riley Raccoon was practicing his tap dance.
   On the big night, Bonnie sang, and then sat down to watch the other animals. "I'm going to win," she said to herself happily. Then the announcer introduced a mystery act. A masked animal came onstage and did a magic show. Hillary looked around. All of her friends were in the audience.

Who could this mystery act be? Write about it below:

_____

_____

_____

_____

_____

_____

_____

_____

_____

0-7424-1801-4 Building Grammar & Writing Skills

Name _____ Date _____

Write a Cinquain

A **cinquain** is a poem with five lines:
- **Line 1** has one word.
- **Line 2** has two words.
- **Line 3** has three words.
- **Line 4** has four or five words.
- **Line 5** has the same word as **Line 1**, or another word that means the same thing.

Read the sample.
Then write a cinquain about one of the subjects below.

sun
hot, yellow
shining all day
keeping earth warm and light
sun

candy	pet	rain
home	**pizza**	**friend**

(candy, home, pet, pizza, rain, friend in bold)

_____

_____

_____

_____

_____

122

   0-7424-1801-4 Building Grammar & Writing Skills

Name _____ Date _____

Rollicking Rhymes

Some poems rhyme.
Read the poem, and fill in the last line with a word that rhymes
with **blue**.

Roses are red
Violets are blue
Sugar is sweet
_____

and so are -- .
_____

Use the words **bright**, **night**, **kite**, **sight**, or **light** to finish the last
two lines of this rhyming poem.

She looked at the star
It was very far

_____
_____
_____
_____

Use the words **jump**, **bump**, **lump**, **stump**, or **thump** to finish the
last two lines of this rhyming poem.

The little green frog
Lived under a log

_____
_____
_____
_____

123

Answer Key

Cuddly Kitty (Page 9) _____

Alphabet Soup (Page 10) _____
ABEGHIKNORSTWY
CDFJLMPQUVXZ

ABC Order (Page 11) _____
apple, boy, cup, duck, egg, fish, girl, hat, ice, jump, king, lip, moon, nut, oak, pen, quick, rat, seed, top, under, van, wish, x-ray, you, zebra

Order, Please! (Page 12) _____
1. bear
2. cat
3. dog

1. bird
2. egg
3. leaves

1. alligator
2. gecko
3. lizard

1. rain
2. snow
3. wind

Next in Line (Page 13) _____
1. cap
2. clown
3. cone

1. fairy
2. feast
3. fish

1. milk
2. moon
3. mud

1. spoon
2. stare
3. swan

In the Beginning (Page 14) _____
cap, sand, dog, franks, mother, girl, beach, hat

Lots of Letters (Page 15) _____
corn, lettuce, tuna, noodles, popcorn, raisins, bread, milk

Spelling Test (Page 16) _____
stars, train, view, wagon, x-ray, yellow, zoo, give

Ending Consonants (Page 17) __
Robert, David, Jeff, Chris, Jordan, Troy, Darryl, Max

At Last (Page 18) _____
pan, clap, skunk, bat, fox, girl, flower

Teamwork Tree (Page 19) _____
1. skunk
2. crayon
3. tree
4. snake
5. broom
6. crab
7. brush
8. skate
9. truck
10. pretty

Perfect Pairs (Page 20) _____
1. flower
2. play
3. flag
4. clock
5. slide
6. sled
7. clock
8. plant
9. climb

Pairing Up (Page 21) _____
cash   thumb   which   sheep
tooth   shoe   bath   chick
wash   chair   with   thorn

Building with Long Vowels (Page 22)
knee   cake   bone
time   use

At the Zoo (Page 23) _____
Color these animals:
zebra   ape   lion   snake
deer   tiger

Short Vowel Search (Page 24) __
Circle these objects:
1. cat, dog
2. hat
3. doll, duck
4. cup
5. pig, hen

Name Game (Page 25) _____
Blue: Cody, James, Kate,
Green: Lin, Brad, Angela, Jenn, Kim

Sneaky, Silent E (Page 26) _____
1. cute
2. mope
3. cane
4. pane
5. bite
6. tube
7. kite
8. cube
9. pine
10. ripe

Fishing for Capitals (Page 27) __
A D F K L Q R S T W X Y

Starting a Sentence (Page 28) __
1. The
2. Anne
3. Do
4. Where
5. Turn
6. Blue
7. My
8. Rain
9. Alan

Capital Reports (Page 29) _____
Rocky Mountains by Ms. Claire Thomas
Main Street by Mr. Raymond Ross

Capital Craze (Page 30) _____
1. Jack and Jill
2. Sports Digest
3. Favorite Fairy Tales
4. Old Yeller
5. Monsters, Inc.
6. Cats and Dogs

Calendar Capitals (Page 31) ____
1. The Science report is due Monday.
2. Tom's birthday is November 4.
3. See Dr. Platt on Wednesday.
4. Soccer practice is changed to Thursday.
5. Our pizza party is on Saturday.
6. Make crafts for Thanksgiving.

Capital Review (Page 32) _____
Jenna's Special Day
Jenna loves to swim. Last Thursday she went with her dad to Clarefield Water Park. They took her best friend Elena. It was very crowded. It was Fourth of July weekend. Elena takes swimming lessons from Mr. Hernandez. She showed Jenna a new stroke. They ate lunch at Pirate Pete's Cove. Jenna had lots of fun. She wants to go back in August.

That's the Point (Page 33) _____
1. Please sit down.
2. John is tired.
4. Eat your dinner.
6. That mouse ate all the cheese.
7. My friends sang a birthday song.
8. I like dinosaurs.
9. Please answer the telephone.

Short and Sweet (Page 34) _____
1. Doctor—Dr.
2. Mister—Mr.
3. January—Jan.
4. Thursday—Thurs.
5. Street—St.
   Sun.—Sunday
   Mon.—Monday
   Tues.—Tuesday
   Wed.—Wednesday
   Thurs.—Thursday
   Fri.—Friday
   Sat.—Saturday

What's the Question? (Page 35)
1. Are you cold?
2. Is that your dog?
5. Who said that?
6. What is your name?

What a Surprise! (Page 36) _____
1. I can't believe we won!
2. Oh no!
4. Wow, I can't believe it!
5. Hooray!
6. Watch out!
9. Be careful!
10. Ouch!

0-7424-1801-4 Building Grammar & Writing Skills

Quote Me (Page 37) _____
1. Eric asked, "What do you want for your birthday?"
2. "I want a new baseball bat," Morgan answered.
3. "I love baseball," said Leo.
4. Emma said, "I'm not surprised."
5. "You play it all the time," added Grant.
6. Eric's mom asked, "Who would like some juice?"
7. "I would," answered Leo.
8. Morgan said, "So would I."
9. "Come to the kitchen," Mom replied.
10. "Okay," everyone said together.

Who Said That? (Page 38) _____
1. Ms. Chaney said, "Class, we have a guest today. This is Officer Dan and his dog Toby."
2. "Hello, class," said Officer Dan.
3. "Hello," the students replied.
4. Officer Dan explained, "I am a police officer. Toby is my partner."
5. Max asked, "Can we pet him?"
6. "Sure," said Officer Dan.
7. "Woof," said Toby.
8. "Did you train Toby?" Bryan asked.
9. "Police dogs have special trainers," Officer Dan replied. "He's a very smart dog."

Mine and Yours (Page 39) _____
1. The bird's nest is high in the tree.
2. Did you see Ryan's puppy?
3. That is the teacher's pen.
4. I rode Sam's bike.
5. The rabbit's ears are very long.
6. Helen's room is blue and white.
7. The book's cover is funny.
8. Tanya's jacket is torn.
9. The dog's coat is shiny.
10. Do you have Rachel's notebook?

Starry Nouns (Page 40) _____
sock, shoe, plant, gift, cherry, water, shell, flag, nest, horse, pool, forest, river, snake

Person, Place, or Thing? (Page 41)
PERSON
grandpa   artist
doctor   teacher
PLACE
beach   park
school   store
THING
snow   book
coat   boots

Who Is It? (Page 42) _____
Answers will vary.

Practice with Nouns (Page 43) ___
1. Jeremy ate a sandwich.
2. The rabbit is brown.
3. Stop. (none)
4. Where is your pencil?
5. Roland is seven years old.
6. Put the book away.
7. You won the game!
8. The fish swam around the pond.
9. Rose was born in Kansas.
10. The wind blew the door open.

Zoo View (Page 44) _____
The lion is like a large cat.
It eats meat.
A lion family is called a pride.
Lion babies are called cubs.

A crocodile is a large reptile.
It lives and hunts in water.
It eats meat.
A crocodile lays eggs.

A giraffe is a mammal.
It is the tallest land mammal.
It eats plants.
The giraffe has long legs and a long neck.

Perfectly Proper (Page 45) _____
dessert— Frosty Yum Ice Cream
country—England
car—Ford
holiday—Valentine's Day
road—Green Road
state—California
song—"Happy Birthday"
movie—Cinderella
book—The Cat in the Hat

More Than One (Page 46) _____
1. birds   2. cats
3. trees   4. gloves
5. crayons   6. eggs
7. cars   8. pictures
9. stars   10. trucks

More Plurals (Page 47) _____
1. glasses   2. matches
3. gases   4. watches
5. taxes   6. brushes
7. switches   8. dresses
9. wishes   10. mixes

Making Plurals (Page 48) _____
shoes, kisses, foxes, lunches, shells, dishes, churches, boxes, pots, patches, chairs, clocks

All About Action (Page 49) _____
1. She hides under the bed.
2. We eat pizza for lunch.
3. I swim on a team.
4. The bunny hops.
5. Gina dances at school.
6. You laugh at everything!
7. Throw your trash in the bin.
8. Emilio swings higher than his brother.
9. I ride my horse every day.
10. Draw a picture of your favorite food.

A Day at the Beach (Page 50) ____
1. Doug and Staci dig in the sand.
2. Wade can build a sandcastle.
3. Emily plays with her puppy.
4. Mom will pour a drink for me.
5. Maddie eats her ice-cream cone.
6. Drew swims in the ocean.

Word Match (Page 51) _____
1. John plays the piano.
2. Beverly wants to go with us.
3. The horse eats hay.
4. Mae bakes cookies.
5. They like chocolate ice cream.
6. The dog barks at the door.
7. The rain hits the window.
8. The team wears red jackets.
9. Cindy never drinks soda.
10. Her parents plant a garden.

Now and Then (Page 52) _____
1. Judy and her sister walk to school. N
2. Regina walked to her friend's house. P
3. Kent watched the parade. P
4. Miguel rides his horse every weekend. P
5. Kerry loved her lost kitten. N
lived, helped, looked, talked, jumped

Being Now (Page 53) _____
1. Jennifer is happy.
2. Rich is wet.
3. Kevin and Todd are asleep.
4. It is raining.
5. Britney is sad.
6. She is wearing a baseball cap.
7. The lions are roaring.
8. I am tired.

Being in the Past (Page 54) _____
1. I was there yesterday.
2. You were working hard.
3. He was afraid of spiders.
4. It was very cold last week.
5. They were riding in the car.
6. Scott was on his skateboard.
7. Yesterday we were in Arizona.
8. Today we are in New Mexico.
9. My sister was a hockey player.
10. My dad and uncle were football players.

0-7424-1801-4 Building Grammar & Writing Skills

Ready for Review (Page 55) _____
Nouns: crayon, leaf, bus, snail, cheese, heart, movie, song
Verbs: think, stand, crawl, yell, throw, cry, push, laugh

Pronoun Power (Page 56) _____
1. <u>We</u> went to the park.
2. <u>He</u> liked it.
3. <u>They</u> are reading.
4. Randy gave it to <u>her</u>.
5. <u>She</u> dropped her doll.

Me, Oh My! (Page 57) _____
1. Circle: I gave
2. Underline: gave her carrot sticks to me
3. Circle: I will go
4. Underline: to the mall with my dad and me
5. Circle: I ate
6. Underline: are good for me
7. Sentences will vary.

Describing Words (Page 58) _____
1. crackling, hot
2. soft, cozy
3. sharp, pointed
4. brave, happy
5. wet, soapy
6. small, fuzzy
7. tired, drowsy
8. crunchy, sweet

Sizes and Shapes (Page 59) _____
Answers will vary.

Colors and Numbers (Page 60) __
snowman, white   cat, black
peas, green   strawberry, red
banana, yellow   book, one
lollipops, two   flowers, three
ribbons, four

Picture This (Page 61) _____
Answers will vary.

Comparing Things (Page 62) ____
1. taller   2. longest
3. brightest   4. smaller
5. smartest   6. higher

Adverb Trees (Page 63) _____
WHEN
weekly   later
yesterday   often
WHERE
under   here
away   nearby
HOW
softly   carefully
loudly   slowly

Ready for Review (Page 64) _____
1. Adjectives: beautiful, pink
2. Adjectives: big, blue; Adverb: slowly.
3. Adjective: new; Adverb: later
4. Adverb: here
5. Adverb: late
6. Adverb: loudly.
7. Adjectives: two happy;
   Adverbs: outside
8. Adverbs: Sometimes, nearby
9. Adjective: red
10. Adjective: nice; Adverb: weekly

I'd Like to Introduce (Page 65) ___
a cat, an egg, a bike, an eye, a fox, an oar, a book, an ax, a fish, a daisy, an ant, an umbrella

More Introductions (Page 66) ___
1. <u>The</u> big, brown horse is very fast.
2. I saw a picture of <u>a</u> horse.
3. A fox is <u>an</u> animal.
4. <u>The</u> blue umbrella is mine.
5. Cleo draws with <u>an</u> orange crayon.
6. George is <u>the</u> class president.
7. My baby brother took a nap.
8. <u>The</u> new puppy chewed on a bone.
9. The teacher spoke to <u>the</u> principal.
10. Today is <u>a</u> sunny day.

Creating Compounds (Page 67) _
1. bedroom   2. fingernail
3. waterfall   4. airplane
5. hallway   6. raindrop
7. sandbox   8. doghouse
9. somebody   10. sunlight

Two Makes One (Page 68) _____
watermelon, raincoat, doorknob, lighthouse, upstairs, pancake, sidewalk, basketball, flowerpot, bluebird

Synonym Seashells (Page 69) __
1. neat—tidy   2. cold—chilly
3. wind—breeze   4. kind—nice
5. plate—dish   6. small—little
7. fluffy—furry   8. mad—angry
9. bark—woof   10. flower—blossom

Tangled Words (Page 70) _____
thin—skinny   laugh—giggle
cry—weep   smile—grin
rip—tear   shout—yell

Silly Sentences (Page 71) _____
1. dry   2. slow
3. short   4. empty
5. up   6. day
7. bottom   8. open
9. huge   10. hate

Opposites Puzzle (Page 72) _____

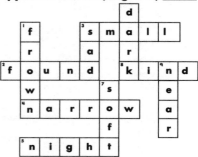

Sound-Alikes (Page 73) _____
1. Brooke has red <u>hair</u>.
   A <u>hare</u> has very long ears.
2. The teacher will <u>meet</u> my parents.
   I love <u>meat</u> and potatoes.
3. Choose the <u>right</u> word.
   I can <u>write</u> the alphabet.
4. The wind <u>blew</u> all day.
   Brianne has <u>blue</u> eyes.
5. Lita has <u>two</u> pencils.
   I want <u>to</u> go <u>too</u>.
6. The apple is <u>red</u>.
   Mom <u>read</u> the book aloud.
7. There was <u>one</u> cookie left.
   Eddie <u>won</u> the race.
8. The puppy liked her <u>new</u> toy.
   Kaitlyn <u>knew</u> the answer.
9. The <u>bee</u> buzzed around the flower.
   I want to <u>be</u> a firefighter.
10. Alexis <u>ate</u> a piece of cake.
    Josh is <u>eight</u> years old.

Matching Sounds (Page 74) ___

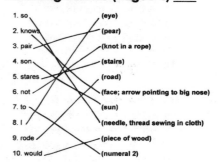

Listen Up! (Page 75) _____
1. tweet
2. meow
3. ring
4. tick-tock
5. boom
6. splat

It Sounds Like (Page 76) _____
Answers will vary.

0-7424-1801-4 Building Grammar & Writing Skills

Rhyme Time (Page 77) _____

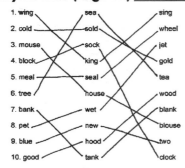

1. wing	sea	sing
2. cold	sold	wheel
3. mouse	sock	jet
4. block	king	gold
5. meal	seal	tea
6. tree	house	wood
7. bank	wet	blank
8. pet	new	blouse
9. blue	hood	two
10. good	tank	clock

Making Contractions (Page 78)
1. he is—he's
2. it is—it's
3. you are—you're
4. we are—we're
5. I am—I'm
6. I will—I'll
7. she will—she'll
8. would not—wouldn't
9. do not—don't
10. are not—aren't

Team Up (Page 79) _____
1. aren't
2. It's
3. won't
4. She's
5. You'll
6. he's
7. can't
8. I'm

Simple Subjects (Page 80) _____
1. I live on River Street.
2. The school band played well.
3. The zoo is open today.
4. The yellow bird sang.
5. Snow and ice covered the road.
6. Angela likes to swim.
7. Andrew's boots are too tight.
8. Claire's bike has a pink basket.
9. A cold wind blew the leaves away.
10. The girls on the soccer team ran fast.

It's All in the Action (Page 81)
1. My pet rabbit eats bananas.
2. Linda brushed her long hair.
3. The teacher wrote on the board.
4. She threw candy into the crowd.
5. George kicked the ball.
6. That sweater is pretty.
7. The artist painted a picture of clouds.
8. The vase broke when it fell.
9. It snowed all night.
10. The ball bounced down the stairs.

Complete Sentences (Page 82) __
1. My favorite shirt is blue.
2. The kitten has striped fur.
3. My horse gallops very fast.
4. I won the baking contest.
5. Some birds fly south for the winter.

It's Not Finished (Page 83) _____
1. The silly clown A
2. Susan and her sister A
3. went to the water park N
4. ran all the way home N
5. My uncle with red hair A
6. likes the lions N
7. The man next door A
8. waits for me N
9. My friend who likes horses A
10. The woman in the blue dress A

Crack the Code (Page 84) _____
1. my friend Jack
2. Lan is happy.
3. Bill likes pie.
4. I ran to the park.
5. the black dog

Tell All About It (Page 85) _____
1. Robyn went to the basketball game.
2. I am thirsty.
3. The room is too cold.
4. My brother Danny likes pizza.
5. Roger ran to school
6. The boy wrote his name on the board.
7. The movie was funny.
8. Paul is a good artist.

I'm Asking (Page 86) _____
1. Who are you?
2. Look at this.
3. Are you six years old?
4. Is that your pencil?
5. I like grapes.
6. Did you hear that?
7. Amy is tired.
8. Mom lost her gloves.
9. What time is it?
10. Tran read the story.

Telling or Asking (Page 87) _____
1. The teddy bear has a big bow.
2. I am six years old.
3. How old are you?
4. My book is blue.
5. Is that your book?
6. John has a puppy.
7. Do you want to play?
8. Did James do his homework?
9. It is raining.
10. Can you run fast?

Make a Change (Page 88) _____
1. Is the balloon red?
2. Do you like pizza?
3. Does he want to run?
4. Is my book here?
5. Will she write the letter?
6. Is the cat striped?

Mix and Match (Page 89) _____
Answers will vary.

Word Scramble (Page 90) _____
1. Horses have long legs.
2. The stars are shining. OR Are the stars shining?
3. I like peanut butter.
4. I won first prize!
5. Is the gate closed? or The gate is closed.
6. Sam and Mike are friends. OR Are Sam and Mike friends?

What's the Idea? (Page 91) _____
The children are feeding the animals.

The Main Idea (Page 92) _____
1. Jordan wants to learn to swim.
2. The bunny wanted to eat carrots.
3. Beverly was a clown for Halloween.

Patrick's Present (Page 93) _____
3—He ran to the living room.
1—Patrick woke up on his birthday.
5—The card said, "Love, Mom and Dad."
6—Patrick thanked his mom and dad with a hug.
2—He jumped out of bed.
4—He found a new bike with a big red ribbon.

Lining Up (Page 94) _____
Andra is third.
Raul is first.
Ashley is second.
Trevor is last.

Costume Party (Page 95) _____

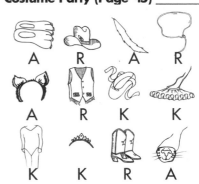

0-7424-1801-4 Building Grammar & Writing Skills

What Doesn't Belong? (Page 97)
dollar bill
pancakes
pencil
sled
flower

Ringed Seals (Page 98) _____
2, 3, 6, 7, 9

Movie Mania (Page 99) _____
Answers will vary.

In the End (Page 100) _____
1. I named my puppy Barney.
2. I could play baseball every day.

Scrambled Sentences (Page 101)
6—But we didn't catch anything.
2—We packed warm clothes and
    sleeping bags.
9—I would like to go camping again.
5—Then we went fishing.
3—We drove to Lake Serenity.

8—The next day was sunny, and we
    went home.
4—When we got to the lake, we put up
    our tent.
1—We went camping last week.
7—It started to rain, so we went to bed
    early.

Fact Find (Page 102) _____
1. True—Snakes are reptiles.
2. False—All snakes are green.
3. True—Snakes shed their skin.
4. True—Some snakes kill prey with
    a bite.
5. False—Some snakes kill prey with
    sharp spikes.
6. False—Snakes never swim.
7. False—Snakes drink milk.
8. True—Most snakes lay eggs.
9. True—Snakes have scales.
10. False—Some snakes have
    small legs.

Organize an Outline (Page 103)
1. Pets
    A. dog
    B. canary
    C. goldfish

2. **Wild animals**
    A. tiger
    B. elephant
    C. polar bear
3. **Farm animals**
    A. cow
    B. chicken
    C. horse

All About Insects (Page 104) ____

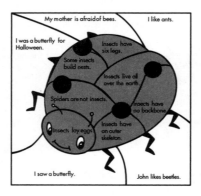

Dear Friend (Page 105) _____
date: April, 7, 2003
greeting: Dear Rebecca,
body of Letter: I had a nice time at your
party. The games were fun. I hope you
had a happy birthday.
closing: Your friend,
name: Wendy

Thank You! (Page 106) _____
Letters will vary.

My Story (Page 107) _____
Autobiographies will vary.

What Do You Think? (Page 108)
1. planting
2. teacher
3. four
4. girl with braids
5. tomatoes

Dear Diary (109) _____
Diary entries will vary.

Write It Right (Page 110)
_____
Jayna was invited to spend the night at
Maria's house. She packed her
toothbrush. Jayna took her favorite doll.
Maria was waiting for her when her
mom dropped her off. "Be a good girl,"
her mom said. She kissed Jayna good-
bye. Maria said, "I am so glad you're
here!" The girls ate pizza. They played
games. Then they went to sleep. Jayna's
mom picked her up the next morning. "I
will invite Maria to our house next
week," Jayna told her mom.

And Then (Page 111)
_____
3—First she jumped up and down in the
    nest.
5—Cleo felt herself rising.
6—She was high above the nest.
7—Cleo was flying!
1—Cleo was a very small bird.
4—Then she opened her wings and
    flapped.
2—She wanted to fly.
Story maps will vary.

Imagine Who (Page 112) _____
Answers will vary.

Imagine Where (Page 113) ____
Answers will vary.

Point of View (Page 114) _____
1. Freddie
2. Corey
3. Gina
4. Rachel

What Comes Next? (Page 115) _
1. The girl with the long hair will win.
2. The glass will break.
3. The water will splash the girl.

Pages (116–124) _____
Answers will vary.

© McGraw-Hill Children's Publishing
0-7424-1801-4 Building Grammar & Writing Skills